Understanding My ADHD

How to Help an ADHD Child
Discover Their Talents,
Improve Executive Functioning Skills and
Develop Coping Mechanisms for ADHD

With 50+ Mindful Activities and ADHD Tools for Kids

Contents

Introduction

ADHD (Attention Deficit Hyperactivity Disorder) can leave you feeling frustrated with the world and sometimes quite lonely too. Don't worry, you have the power to turn ADHD into something very positive!

Take a moment to breathe in slowly through your nose and out through your mouth, then relax your shoulders.

Today is the day you say a big 'hello' to some different feelings, much better feelings! This is the day you start to learn about *your* ADHD. You will discover the things your brain loves, what it finds most challenging and how your incredible brain can help you on the path to success!

Using fun facts, inspirational stories and easy to follow examples, you are starting on a journey of self-discovery to find out what ADHD means for you. With a huge focus on positivity you will uncover important skills and simple ways of helping you manage the challenges of ADHD so you can take control of everyday frustrations and succeed.

This educational activity book is filled with lots of helpful tips and practical exercises to help you grow in confidence and be at your very best at home, in school and with your friends.

Inside this book you will find lively pictures to color in. This is a good opportunity for you to take a break, absorb the information you have learned and enjoy some relaxation time. Coloring in the pictures can also mark where you are in your ADHD journey. We suggest you use coloring pencils, not felt tip pens, so it's easier to read what's on the other side.

If you are a younger reader, or you need a little help, it may be a good idea to ask an adult to read through all or parts of this book with you. Perhaps you might enjoy some help to work through some of the exercises and activities too.

Right now, you may feel a little overwhelmed at the thought of learning all about ADHD and how to manage it, but don't worry, this book will break down each step into easy bite sized chunks which you can work through at your own pace.

However scary it may feel at times, remember that by starting this book you have taken a brilliant first step in beginning to understand your ADHD. The skills you learn in this book will help you to feel happy and do well, not only now but throughout your whole life.

So…take a deep breath, remind yourself how great you are and let's begin to find out all about you and your fantastic brain…

ONE

Understanding What ADHD Means for Me

YOU ARE A UNIQUE INDIVIDUAL. You may experience ADHD differently from other people. This is because ADHD behaviors (symptoms) exist on a spectrum. A spectrum is a scale, which is different at each end; some people may experience lots of symptoms and some people may have just a few.

Not everyone with ADHD experiences the same symptoms. For instance, some people may find ADHD makes them hyperactive and they can't sit still. For others, ADHD means they have trouble paying attention for longer stretches of time. Still, others experience both of these symptoms and any number of other symptoms in between. Not only do people with ADHD have different symptoms, people experience them at different levels of intensity as well.

So, if there are so many different symptoms, how will you

be able to figure out what's causing the challenges you experience every day? Don't worry. This book will help you find out.

Did you know ADHD can be a good thing? No? Well, it's true. In fact, ADHD might make you better at some things! For instance, people with ADHD are known to be more creative. This is because the way your brain is made likely makes you better at thinking "outside of the box." The "outside of the box" thinking allows you to come up with unique ideas and ways of expressing yourself that wouldn't happen to other people. Maybe your English teacher has described your writing as imaginative. Or your art teacher says your use of color is revolutionary. ADHD might be the reason you're so good at these creative activities.

ADHD gives you many incredible skills. We like to call these skills *"Super Skills!"*

Your Super Skills are amazing. There are so many incredible things you can do because of ADHD. Here are just a few ADHD Super Skills:

- **Adventurous**: People with ADHD are sometimes impulsive. They tend to do things on the spur of the moment. This makes being around them fun and exciting! Are you the first of your friends to ride on a scary Ferris wheel? You can probably thank ADHD for making you adventurous. People will enjoy being around you if you have this Super Skill.

- **Entrepreneurial:** This is said about business people who gain success by taking risks and managing enterprises. Being more likely to take risks, people with ADHD tend to do very well as entrepreneurs. In fact, they are three times more likely to become entrepreneurs!

- **Energetic**: Hyperactivity means having lots of energy. With this Super Skill, you could reach the top of your field in any sport.

- **Generosity**: ADHD helps some people become more caring. As ADHD can be challenging at times, it makes you better able to understand other people's struggles and want to help them.

Having ADHD means your brain works a little differently to other people's brains. Learning about how your unique brain works will help you overcome the obstacles you face. Of course, you will also learn about how your individual brain gives you Super Skills!

Let's try to figure out what some of your challenges are. Try to think about how your ADHD makes your life harder. What are some of the things you find difficult? Below are some examples of what some of these challenges might be.

1. Trouble listening in class
2. Difficulty in sitting still
3. Struggling to let others finish speaking
4. Difficulty in concentrating when reading
5. Struggling to get up in the morning
6. Difficulty in thinking before acting

Now see if you can come up with some of your own examples:

1.

2.

3.

4.

5.

6.

7.

It may seem like your list is long, but don't worry, this book will help you figure out how to overcome these challenges. The first step in fixing challenges is being able to identify them. Well done! You've taken the first step to overcoming your obstacles.

Now that you've identified some of your challenges, let's see if you can figure out what your Super Skills are. Here are a few examples of what some of these might be:

1. The ability to see other people's point of view
2. Exercising without getting tired
3. Caring about other people
4. Writing imaginative stories
5. Making people laugh

Now, see if you can come up with some of your own examples:

1.

2.

3.

4.

5.

6.

7.

Are you surprised by how many Super Skills you have? Do you know a lot of people have these skills as a result of ADHD? ADHD is not that rare. Of the world's 7.8 billion people, 5–8% have ADHD. That's up to nearly 700 million people!

So, you are not alone. Of course, not everyone experiences ADHD exactly the way you do. Some people have few symptoms that don't bother them too much. Other people have lots of symptoms and they sometimes struggle. Wherever you fit on the ADHD spectrum, this book will help you overcome your challenges and maximize your Super Skills.

Speaking of Super Skills, did you know there are quite a few famous people who have ADHD? Have you heard of any of them? Can you guess who they might be?

Now that you know about Super Skills, you might be able to guess which celebrities have ADHD.

Read on to find out which of your favorite celebrities have ADHD just like you do!

Chapter Summary

- ADHD is a spectrum and people experience a range of symptoms.
- Figuring out how ADHD challenges you will help you to overcome obstacles.
- ADHD can be positive too, giving you amazing Super Skills!
- Hundreds of millions of people experience ADHD.

In the next chapter you will learn....

- Why it can be hard for you to focus.
- Lots of ways to help you focus.
- The ability to recognize when you might face challenges to your focus in order to stop them from becoming a problem.

TWO

Fixing My Focus

LET'S FACE IT, it can be hard for many children to focus. However, for a child with ADHD, it can be *really* hard to focus. ADHD makes it hard for some children to concentrate on the task at hand, especially if it's not very exciting.

The parts of the brain that deal with attention work a little differently for you. This means you may become easily distracted by things going on around you. It's not that you don't want to pay attention to what you're supposed to be doing, it's just that your brain isn't made to stay on one task easily.

Even though it's not your fault that you find it difficult to focus, it's natural for you to become frustrated when you struggle to do so.

It can be annoying when everyone else around you finds

it easy to focus and you can't stop yourself from being distracted. You may feel like you're always getting into trouble for not listening to instructions.

Sometimes this means you make mistakes, or forget things. For instance, when your teacher asks you why you aren't paying attention in class, it may make you feel embarrassed or even ashamed. You weren't trying to lose focus on purpose, so your teacher's response may even make you feel annoyed or angry.

These are all perfectly normal reactions to a situation you can't control. Sometimes you may feel like your emotions get the better of you when you struggle to focus, which can make you feel even worse! In order to help you through these emotions, it's important for you to be able to identify them.

One of the best ways that you can get to the bottom of your emotions is for you to talk about them. Speaking about our emotions aloud helps us to face them, rather than keeping them inside.

When we describe our emotions, we have to think about how we feel when we are upset. This, in turn, allows us to figure out the underlying feelings that are behind the emotions. For instance, we might cry when we're emotional. Sometimes crying means we're sad. Other times it means we're angry.

Think about how you feel when you cry. What else are you feeling? Are your fists balled? Are you clenching your teeth? This might mean you are not just sad, but also angry.

Once you know *what* you are feeling when you're emotional, then you can figure out the cause.

Do you know why you might be angry? Perhaps it's because you couldn't sit still when you were meant to be focusing on a task.

Think about some of the occasions when you struggled with focusing. What emotions did you feel at that time?

Try to list some of the emotions you had:

1.

2.

3.

4.

5.

6.

7.

If you have trouble thinking of what your emotions were, try to think about how you expressed your emotions. Did you ball your fists or shout? Maybe you were feeling angry. Did your heart race or were you struggling to breathe? Maybe you were feeling anxious or worried. Did you struggle to hold in your tears? Maybe you were sad.

It can be upsetting when you struggle to focus. It's understandable that you would feel emotional. But don't be afraid, we have some ways to try to help you learn to focus.

- Break tasks into smaller chunks. For instance, if you have to write a book report, break it down into smaller topics or paragraphs. Taking short breaks between 'chunks' will enable you to recharge your focus.

During the break, try to do something relaxing and enjoyable. Perhaps you could try something physical, to help you get rid of excess energy. Make sure to set a time limit on these breaks in case you end up being distracted from your original task for too long.

- Give yourself rewards. If you have something positive to look forward to, this will spur you on to continue with your task. The greater the reward, the greater the motivation for you to stay focused. If you're having an especially difficult time staying on task, choose something you really enjoy as a reward, such as an hour playing your favorite video game.

- Use a fidget aid. Some people with ADHD benefit from using physical aids, like fidget spinners, to stop their attention from wandering.

Fidget aids help burn excess energy and also relieve boredom and a lack of focus just enough to keep you on task. If fidget spinners aren't your thing, there are various fidget aids you can try, like stress balls, knuckle bones, or even playdough. If it keeps your hands busy, try it.

- Listen to music. Music can help you filter out other distractions by helping certain parts of your brain relax. You can tailor the music to suit your mood. If you're feeling tired, try some uplifting music. If you are having trouble sitting still, try some calming music.

- Exercise while working. If you simply have too much energy to sit still and work, try combining a physical activity with the task you want to focus on. Sitting on a medicine ball instead of a chair may be enough to contain your energy as you try to stay balanced while you sit.

There are a variety of seated exercise machines you could try to keep yourself busy while you work. For instance, seated foot pedals and exercisers can be used. Vibration machines might also help. The physical vibration that moves your body could calm the urge to move, as well as soothe and calm your mind.

Try the above tasks to see which ones work for you. Don't feel bad if not all of them work. Different things work for different people.

Maybe you already have a few solutions to keep yourself focused. Or maybe the above solutions have given you a few ideas of your own.

Activity:

Write down your ideas about how to stay focused:

1.

2.

3.

4.

5.

6.

7.

Daily Activity: Have a Go

Next time you have difficulty staying focused and experience the emotions you listed above, try one of the solutions we suggested, or one of your own ideas.

The table below shows you how you might record what happens.

Day	Cause	Emotion	Solution	Did it work?
Monday	My sister wouldn't let me play with her.	Annoyed and frustrated	Use a fidget object (stress ball).	Yes, I felt calmer and could concentrate.
Tuesday	My Mom got annoyed because I forgot to do the dishes.	Sad	Listen to music (upbeat).	I felt a bit less sad.
Wednesday	I had too much homework and didn't know where to start.	Worried	Break tasks into smaller chunks.	I felt much calmer.

Over the next week, try this exercise each day using the table below.

Daily Activity:

Day	Cause	Emotion	Solution	Did It Work?
Monday				
Tuesday				
Wednesday				
Thursday				
Friday				
Saturday				

Weekly Activity:

Over the week, try to see if you can figure out what causes challenges to your focus. Over time, you might start to see a pattern. For instance, have you found that a loud classmate distracts you with their noisy talking?

Now that you know the cause of your challenge, you can think of a way to stop it from occurring. Perhaps you could move to a different seat, for example.

When you manage to take steps to correct the cause of your challenges, write down what happened. By the end of the week, you should have a list of changes you have made. Isn't it awesome that you've managed to make life easier for yourself? You should feel proud of yourself! Show a parent or teacher your list. Talk to them about your feelings.

Did You Know...?

Did you know that Michael Phelps has ADHD? He is quite possibly the most famous Olympic medalist of all time, with the most gold medals ever won by an individual.

When he was younger, Michael thought he wouldn't get anywhere in life. He couldn't sit still in class and struggled to listen to the teacher.

Then, one day he got into the water and suddenly, he was able to think clearly. His hyperactivity gave him more energy than most swimmers, which is probably one of the reasons that he managed to become the best in the world at it!

Chapter Summary

- Your brain works a little differently which can make it hard for you to focus.
- Identifying your emotions will help you figure out what causes you to lose focus.
- There are many ways of helping you overcome the challenges which stop you from focusing.

In the next chapter you will learn....

- How your ADHD affects your ability to make decisions and exercise self-control.
- Lots of ways to help you make good decisions and stay in control.
- How to anticipate challenges, so you can prevent them from becoming a problem.

THREE

Making Great Decisions and Learning Self-Control

YOUR IMPULSIVITY MEANS you sometimes do things without thinking them through first.

The part of your brain that controls decision-making works a little differently. It's sometimes harder for you to know which decisions are better in the long run. Often, you might do something because it seems like it's more exciting or easier rather than it being the best option.

Your impulsivity may get in the way of your social life. For instance, you may find it difficult not to interrupt people when they are talking to you. Because your brain works quickly, with lots of thoughts popping into your head, it may be hard for you to let the other person finish what they have to say. This can make people frustrated with you, which can be upsetting for both you and them.

What are some of the emotions you have when you face the challenge of making good decisions?

You might feel sad because your friend doesn't want to hang around with you as much because you keep interrupting. You are probably frustrated because you don't want to interrupt, but it feels like you can't stop yourself.

Try to write down some of the emotions you feel when you struggle with making decisions and staying in control:

1.

2.

3.

4.

5.

6.

7.

How do you feel when you think about these emotions? It's not nice when you feel like you can't control your own behavior or make the right choices.

Don't worry though, we have some possible solutions for you to try that might help you make good decisions and learn self-control:

- Before making a decision, write down a list of different actions you could take. Think about each one carefully and decide on the one that suits the situation best. Line the good and bad of each decision up against each other.

- To help stop interrupting people, practice your listening skills. For instance, show an interest in the other person's situation by asking questions. Practice with your family.

- If it's a big decision, try to gather information before deciding on what to do. For instance, if you want to buy a tablet, don't make a snap decision. Research which one will suit you best. If you want to take great photos, you need a device that can do this.

- Talk to someone you trust before making a decision or taking an action you're unsure about. Your parents, brothers, sisters, or a trusted family friend may be good people to talk through your options without feeling judged.

- Before you make a decision or give in to an impulse, pause to give yourself a chance to think first. Try counting to ten before you act, so you can avoid doing the first thing that comes to mind.

Activity:

You might be able to think of other possible solutions you can try to help you with self-control and making decisions. Give it a go. We bet you have some good ideas!

1.

2.

3.

4.

5.

6.

7.

Daily Activity: Have a Go

Next time you have difficulty with the challenge of making a decision or controlling your impulses, try some of the activities listed above. Below is an example of how you might record what happens.

Day	Cause	Emotion	Solution	Did it Work?
Monday	Stopping myself from disrupting class by talking over the teacher.	Stressed by my need to talk	Count to ten before I act.	Yes. By the time I counted to ten, the moment passed and I no longer felt the urge to speak out loud anymore.
Tuesday	Deciding on whether to go to the movies or study.	Confused and conflicted	Think about the good (pros) and bad (cons) of each alternative.	Yes, the cons of not studying outweigh the pros of going to the movies.
Wednesday	Choosing which shoes to buy.	Overwhelmed	Do my homework to figure out which is the best brand.	Yes. The shoes I originally wanted were cheaper, but they had bad reviews and did not last long. I decided on the more expensive ones that'll last longer.
Thursday	Deciding whether to go for a bike ride without my helmet.	Excited about biking but worried about getting hurt	Weigh up the options with pros and cons.	Yes. I decided it was better to avoid going for a bike ride because the risk of falling off the bike without a helmet was not worth it.

Once you have tried the solutions for yourself, fill out the table below to see which ones were successful for you.

Day	Cause	Emotion	Solution	Did it Work?
Monday				
Tuesday				
Wednesday				
Thursday				
Friday				
Saturday				
Sunday				

Over the week, when you find yourself in a situation that challenges your ability to make a decision and control yourself, see if you can anticipate the challenge and prevent it from being a problem.

For instance, if you are with your friends, are you more likely to find making decisions challenging, or are you more likely to have less self-control?

Perhaps you are more likely to take risks when you're with your friends. Are there times when you find some challenges more difficult? For instance, during the weekend, when you are at home, do you tend to eat too much junk food?

Now that you're beginning to predict when a challenge might occur, you should be able to come up with a solution to stop it from happening.

For instance, when you are hungry during the weekend, try to set out some healthy snacks so you don't end up eating too much junk food. Or, if your friends are about to do something that might have bad results, you can see this ahead of time and come up with an alternate solution for them. For instance, you could come up with something that won't have bad results.

Activity:

Make a list of all the times you managed to avoid the negative outcomes of your challenges by thinking about them ahead of time.

1.

2.

3.

4.

5.

6.

7.

You've probably come up with quite a long list of successes! Well done! Think about sharing this list with a teacher or a parent. They will probably be impressed and may have some ideas to help you anticipate future challenges.

Did You Know...?

Did you know that musician Mel B has ADHD? The successful singer and television personality says she uses exercise to help her with her symptoms, enabling her to focus. Even the rich and famous need to use strategies to help them overcome their individual ADHD issues, just like you!

Chapter Summary

- Impulsivity means that making good decisions and having self-control are difficult for people with ADHD.
- There are many possible solutions to help you with the challenge of making good decisions. For example, making a pros and cons list will help you choose your actions wisely.
- Anticipating challenges to making good decisions and controlling yourself will help you stop them from becoming problems.

In the next chapter you will learn....

- Why regulating emotions is difficult for people with ADHD.
- To identify the feelings you have when you struggle with emotions in order to help you stop them from becoming a problem.
- Strategies to help you with the challenge of your emotions.

FOUR

Getting to Grips with My Emotions

EMOTIONS MAY BE CHALLENGING for you because emotions can be difficult for people with ADHD to control. It may be hard for people with ADHD to figure out how much is the appropriate amount of emotion to feel in different situations.

For instance, some people with ADHD find themselves getting just as upset over small things, like getting a paper cut, as they do over bigger things, like dropping an expensive laptop and breaking it.

You may also have trouble controlling your emotions overall as a result of ADHD. You might feel happy one moment and upset the next without knowing why.

Please remember, it's not all bad. Your strong emotions mean you feel things deeply. You care about people and you're aware of their feelings. This is actually a Super

Skill! Being able to see things from other people's perspective is a rare ability and you probably have it naturally. We bet your friends and family are glad you have this Super Skill.

A good way for you to figure out what it is that you're feeling when your emotions are challenging is to write down exactly what you're feeling. For instance, were you angry all of a sudden when someone accidentally bumped into you? What did you feel when that happened? Did your heart race? Did you raise your voice or stomp your feet? Did you feel out of control?

Sometimes when we're upset, our emotions cause us to express this physically. When it comes to ADHD, people often feel stronger emotions than the situation calls for. This is natural because ADHD makes it difficult for people to judge their feelings and respond accordingly.

Try to write exactly what you feel when you are challenged by your emotions.

1.

2.

3.

4.

5.

6.

7.

Some of those emotions can seem overwhelming and frightening. You probably don't like it when you're angry and upset. Well, we have some possible solutions that might help you address the challenge of your emotions.

- **Try to rate the situation that caused your emotional response.** Rate the situation as either annoying, upsetting, or intolerable. For instance, getting a papercut would be rated as annoying, while having your bike stolen would be upsetting. Learning to rate situations for how upsetting they are can teach you to regulate your emotional response to them.

- **Think again about the situation.** When you get upset, it might be because you have jumped to the wrong conclusion. For instance, let's say your phone went missing. Last time you saw it, your friend was playing with it. You immediately get angry thinking your friend either lost it or stole it.

Before you respond, reassess the situation. What if he gave it back to you and you forgot? What if he did accidentally drop it? He didn't do it on purpose. If you talk to your friend, he may be able to help you retrace your steps and find it.

- **Try to use mindfulness when you feel yourself getting emotional**. Mindfulness is a form of meditation that helps you live in the moment. An easy way to use mindfulness is in your breathing. Breathing in slowly and being aware of your breath can help to control your emotions. Holding your breath and breathing out slowly will help you calm down and it will slow down your thinking.

If you do this each day, it will help regulate your emotions overall. Getting good at this technique means you will be able to use it quickly when you need to control your emotions.

- **Practice expressing your feelings.** If you are upset with someone, don't immediately confront them. Imagine talking to them. Tell them how you're feeling. Now, imagine how they would reply.

Doing this will show you their perspective and help you understand the reason for whatever made you upset.

When you do approach them to discuss the problem, you will be calm enough to hear them.

- **Role play.** If you get upset with certain situations, get a trusted adult or family friend to roleplay your reactions with you. Have the other person take your side of the situation. This will show you different ways to respond emotionally.

- **Write a diary.** This can help you sort through your emotions. Write freely, as if you are talking to a friend.

Once you have everything down on paper, return when you are calmer. Reading your emotions when you feel differently can give you perspective. You will hopefully understand your emotions better, which will help you regulate them in the future.

- **Giving the emotion a name** and saying it out loud to yourself can really help. For example, you might say "I am worried" and then tell yourself why you are worried.

This is a particularly useful exercise if there is no one you can share your feelings with at the time.

- **Try to redirect your emotions**. If you are angry, listen to music. Dance wildly to let off steam, or sing loudly to your favorite song.

Letting go of your emotions before they take over can teach you how to regulate them.

By cutting your emotions off before they get out of control, you've taught yourself a new response.

- **Use fidget objects to calm yourself.** Using a stress ball helps bring down your heart rate and distract you from extreme emotions.

This is the first step in learning how to control your emotions.

- **Talk to someone you trust**, like a family member or friend. Tell them all about your emotions. See if they can help you understand why you feel the way you do.

They can reassure and calm you, which will teach you how to be calm in future.

- **Use color therapy.** ADHD makes you more sensitive to the things you see, hear, and feel. Colors can affect people's moods and their thoughts. People with ADHD are said to be more sensitive to the effects of colors on the mind. For instance, blue, green, grey and violet can be calming.

Look at the colors on the front of this book. These colors are especially useful at reducing hyperactivity in children with ADHD. Perhaps you could talk to your parents about painting your bedroom in one of these cooler, calming colors, which would be especially useful when you need to concentrate and remain calm.

Reds, yellows, and oranges are stimulating, which may actually not be good for you if you're having a tough time sitting still or being calm.

Are there any other solutions that you can think of? Maybe this list has given you some different ideas about how to face the challenge of your emotions.

Activity:

Write down some of your solutions to emotional challenges:

1.

2.

3.

4.

5.

6.

7.

You've probably come up with some amazing ideas, or maybe there are some solutions you've already tried that have worked for you. Well done!

Daily Activity: Have a Go

Now, see if you can use some of the strategies we've discussed to help with the challenge of regulating your emotions.

In the table below are some examples of how you might do this:

Day	Cause	Emotion	Strategy	Did it Work?
Monday	I got angry when my friend ignored my phone call. I thought she didn't want to be friends anymore.	Angry	Think about the situation again. Maybe she couldn't answer my call.	Yes, it turned out her phone died. When I saw her the next day, she explained everything.
Tuesday	I got upset when the teacher called me out in class for forgetting my homework. I felt like crying.	Upset, sad, embarrassed	Mindful breathing.	A bit. It calmed me down and stopped me from crying.

Now try this out for yourself by filling out the table below:

Day	Cause	Emotion	Strategy	Did It Work?
Monday				
Tuesday				
Wednesday				
Thursday				
Friday				
Saturday				
Sunday				

Have you figured out which strategies worked for you? Good on you!

Weekly Activity:

As you spend your week using different strategies to overcome the challenge you face regulating your emotions, try to see if there are any patterns in your behavior. For instance, do you find your emotions are worse at the end of the day? Perhaps you are hungry or tired. Try eating something, or do some mindful breathing to re-energize.

Over the week you've probably managed to anticipate many of the emotional challenges before they happen and you've been able to stop them from being a problem. Good job!

Why don't you write a list of the times when you managed to pre-empt your emotional challenges and stop them in their tracks?

1.

2.

3.

4.

5.

6.

7.

You've probably written quite a list. You're making such good progress! It's probably time to share your success with a parent or teacher. They will be pleased with how you're doing and may have more ideas about how you can continue to stop your challenges from becoming big issues.

Did You Know…?

Speaking of successful people, singer and actor Adam Levine had trouble memorizing songs because of his ADHD. He has since reached fame as an actor, record producer and television host.

It's beginning to seem like people who have reached worldwide fame and success have something in common, isn't it? All of these people who have ADHD are creative and successful. They have not let their symptoms slow them down, and neither should you!

Chapter Summary

- ADHD makes it difficult for people to regulate their emotions.
- There are many ways to help with the challenge of emotions. For instance, meditation can help you calm your emotions.

- Using different tips and tricks you can recognize situations that make emotional control difficult, which will allow you to control your emotions before they become a problem.

In the next chapter you will learn....

- How ADHD makes people hyperactive.
- Different ways to help you overcome the challenge of hyperactivity.
- How to recognize when you are likely to be challenged by hyperactivity in order to stop it from being a problem.

FIVE

Staying Still with Ease

IT CAN FEEL like it's impossible to sit still when you have ADHD. It's not just that you would rather be moving, it's that you can't stop yourself. Hyperactivity is one of the main symptoms of ADHD. Your ADHD makes it difficult for you to sit still sometimes. You might see this in a number of ways. You could start fidgeting or squirming in your seat. Do you ever find yourself talking too much?

All of these things are perfectly normal behaviors for someone with ADHD, though they may not make you feel normal. Although it's not your fault, you've probably gotten into trouble for being unable to fight the urge to move.

People might think you're being disruptive on purpose, or that you're trying to get attention. It must be so frustrating for you! It's natural for you to get upset when this happens. After all, being hyperactive can be quite exhausting. It's normal to feel frustrated and upset when your behavior isn't something you can control.

What other emotions do you have when you struggle to be still or remain quiet? You might feel embarrassed. If no one else is moving but you can't stop squirming, people might not understand. If the teacher tells you off for speaking out of turn or moving in your seat, you may feel ashamed because everyone is looking at you.

Can you think of any other feelings you have when your hyperactivity is a challenge? Try to write some of these feelings down:

1.

2.

3.

4.

5.

6.

7.

Those are a lot of emotions to have. You must be frustrated. Not to worry! We have some possible solutions that might help you with the challenge of staying still.

- **Exercise** is the perfect way for you to burn off extra energy. Exercising can take away the feeling of being hyperactive, enabling you to concentrate and sit still when you need to. Try to choose a physical hobby or sport that is fun.

Can you think of something you've always wanted to try? Is there a sport you already enjoy? If you know you are going to be in a position where you have to sit still for long periods, why not burn off some energy first. If sitting in class is difficult, perhaps you can walk to school. If you're not old enough to do this by yourself, try asking a parent or an older sibling or friend you trust to walk with you.

- Sometimes sights and sounds around you draw your focus away, making you feel restless and bringing on your hyperactivity. Try to **minimize interruptions** to your attention by removing yourself from them.

For instance, if what's happening outside draws your attention and makes sitting still harder, ask your teacher if you can move to a seat away from the window.

- **Use fidget aids.** They are the best thing to use up distracting energy without having to remove yourself from a situation. Exercise helps the best, but you can't very well go for a run when you're meant to be in class!

A fidget object is the next best thing. It will keep your hands busy, taking away just enough of the urge to move to allow you to sit still.

- **Try body scanning.** Body scanning is a mindfulness or meditation form. You can use it in a situation where you need to be still, like in the classroom. Start at your toes and squeeze them before letting go. Move onto your legs and squeeze those muscles before moving up to your thighs.

When you release the squeeze, think of that body part staying still. Continue throughout your body. At first, body scanning will take effort, but as you practice, it will become easy. It will soon become second nature and you will be able to do it easily. Body scanning works, because when you release the squeeze it makes your body and your mind feel relaxed, helping to still your hyperactivity.

- If hyperactivity makes you talk too much or interrupt people, try to **delay speaking**. Count to ten if you feel yourself wanting to talk when you are meant to be quiet. Counting to ten will

focus your attention and still your thoughts
enough to calm your hyperactivity.

You may like to ask someone you trust to remind you to count when your hyperactivity affects your speech. You may not know you are talking too much or at the wrong time. Your parents, other members of your family, or a teacher may be able to give you a gentle reminder. Don't be afraid to ask for help. If people know you are struggling, they will be more understanding.

Activity:

You may already have some ideas of your own to help you when hyperactivity becomes too much for you. Write down some of these and any other ideas you have for helping you with the challenge of keeping still.

1.

2.

3.

4.

5.

6.

7.

You've probably come up with a great list of ideas. Well done! You're really getting the hang of this. Now, let's see if you can put these ideas into action:

Daily Activity: Have a Go

The table below shows you examples of how you might use these ideas:

Day	Cause	Emotion	Strategy	Did it Work?
Monday	I kicked my legs, bumping the desk in front of me by mistake, upsetting the child in front.	Frustrated, energetic	Body scan.	Yes, it was hard at first, but as I squeezed different parts of my body and let the pressure go, I felt the need to kick my legs decrease.
Tuesday	I started to hum to myself in class without realizing it and the teacher told me to stop.	Embarrassed	Fidget Aid	Yes, I used my fidget spinner and it stopped me from humming.
Wednesday	I kept interrupting my Mom when she was talking about her day during dinner.	Excitable and hyperactive	Counting for ten seconds	Yes. At first it was hard because I kept wanting to speak, but then the more I stopped myself by counting, the easier it was to let my Mom finish speaking.

See if you can try this activity yourself by filling out the table below:

Day	Cause	Emotion	Strategy	Did It Work?
Monday				
Tuesday				
Wednesday				
Thursday				
Friday				
Saturday				
Sunday				

Hopefully this exercise has helped you identify which strategies work for you. Good on you! Keep up the good work.

Weekly Activity:

As you try some of the strategies we've discussed to help you with the challenge of staying still, you may have noticed some patterns. Are there times when you're more likely to find hyperactivity challenging? Is it first thing in the morning, when you have to sit still in class? Do you become more hyperactive toward the end of the school day, waiting for the bell to ring? Perhaps you've even managed to stop your challenge before it becomes a problem.

We bet that if you wrote a list of the times when you managed to stop the challenge of keeping still before it became too much, you might be surprised by how well you've done. Give it a try now.

1.

2.

3.

4.

5.

6.

7.

How does it feel to have stopped hyperactivity before it gets really bad? You should feel good about yourself! Let your parents or teacher know how well you're doing by showing them the list.

Did You Know...?

Did you know home improvement star Ty Pennington struggled with hyperactivity as a child, which led him to distracting his fellow classmates? It wasn't until he discovered a talent for art that Ty realized he could put this to use.

If you struggle with hyperactivity, remember Ty Pennington and the fact that you are not alone in your struggle. Like with Ty Pennington, your hyperactivity may turn out to be one of your Super Skills. Never think your ADHD will stop you from achieving your goals.

Chapter Summary

- Hyperactivity is a symptom of ADHD. It can cause you to have trouble sitting still. It can also cause you to interrupt other people when they are talking.
- There are many ways to help you with the challenge of being hyperactive, including the use of fidget toys to help use up energy.

- Figuring out when hyperactivity may occur allows you to stop it from happening.

In the next chapter you will learn....

- Why being on time is a challenge for people with ADHD.
- Strategies to help you with the challenge of being on time.
- How to figure out when being on time might be a challenge for you so you can make sure it isn't a problem.

SIX

All in Good Time

BEING ON TIME IS HARD. It's difficult for people with ADHD to remember all of the things they need to do in order to get out of the door on time. With so many fun distractions going on around you, it's easy for you to go off track.

You probably find you're always late for class. Your parents are probably constantly having to chase you up to get things done on time. It's not nice to feel like you're always being nagged. You probably wonder why you can't just be on time like everyone else. It's not your fault that your brain misjudges the time and is distracted, but you can work to improve your ability to be on time, for everything!

How else does your struggle with being on time make you feel? Do you feel stressed because you are always rushing until the last minute? Do you feel embarrassed about walking into a room late, and have everyone staring at you?

Activity:

What other feelings do you have when you struggle with being on time? Write down as many of these that you can think of below:

1.

2.

3.

4.

5.

6.

7.

It must be difficult for you to struggle to be on time no matter how hard you try. Well, don't feel down. Here are some things for you to try that may help.

- **Make a wall chart.** This will help you do things at a specific time of day and keep you on time. On the chart, write down everything you need to do before you leave the house in the morning. Start with breakfast, brushing your teeth and placing your lunch in your backpack.

Once you've done a task, tick it off the list; that way you will know what you have to do next. Include the tasks you need to do after school as well, including homework and any chores.

Getting to bed on time is really important so write down everything you need to do before bed too. If you find your attention wandering when you should be getting ready, set an alarm or timer to help you stay on track. You could set an alarm ten minutes before it's time to leave. This way, you know exactly how long you have before you need to be out the door. If you still find yourself rushing, set several alarms, one half an hour before you need to leave and another one ten minutes before you need to leave.

- **Ask for help.** If you find yourself daydreaming or taking too long with one task, ask a parent or family member to help. They can remind you to keep getting ready to ensure you are on time.

- **Prepare the night before.** If you are still struggling to get ready on time, try preparing things in advance of when you need them. For example, pack your homework and your gym kit in your bag the night before, so you don't have to find them in the morning. Make your lunch the night before and place it in the fridge, so it's ready to grab first thing in the morning.

Pop a note on the front door to remind you that your lunch is in the fridge so you don't forget it. Decide what you're going to wear the night before and lay it out ready to wear the next day.

- **Wake up earlier.** If you still can't get everything done in time, you might need to wake up a little earlier. In order for this to work, you'll need a good night of sleep, which means going to bed a little earlier.

Try setting an alarm to remind you that it's nearly time for bed, so you know it's time to start preparing for sleep.

- **Don't do too many things at once.** If you find yourself running late all the time, it might be that you're doing too much.

For example, if you have a lot of homework to do, but you decide to spend the day visiting friends, that may mean you could end up doing homework late. That will mean you get to bed late, and then you won't be able to get up on time.

- **Remove distractions.** If you have homework or chores to do, try to keep distractions out of reach. Place your devices in another room while doing homework, so you aren't tempted to read messages or check on social media when you are meant to be working.

This will mean you can complete work quicker, leaving you with more time for the other things you want and need to do.

Activity:

What other solutions to the challenge of being on time can you think of? Write them down below:

1.

2.

3.

4.

5.

6.

7.

That's heaps of ideas. Way to go!

Daily Activity: Have a Go

When you experience some of those emotions you identified that occur as a result of your struggle with being on time try to use one of the strategies above.

In the table below is an example of how you might record this activity:

Day	Cause	Emotion	Strategy	Did it Work
Monday	I slept in, so I ended up rushing and forgot to pack my lunch.	Panic	Prepare the night before and leave a note on the front door	Yes, I made my lunch the night before and the note on the door reminded me to take it from the fridge.
Tuesday	I got distracted streaming a movie and I went to bed too late.	Disappointment in myself	Make a wall chart	Yes, the wall chart reminded me to do my homework, chores and bedtime preparation, which stopped me watching the movie for too long.
Wednesday	I was meant to go to soccer practice but ended up late because I was hanging out with friends beforehand.	Stressed	Don't do too much.	Yes, when my friends asked me to hang out, I told them I couldn't because of soccer practice. I ended up going to soccer on time.

See if you can try this for yourself. Record your results in the table below.

Day	Cause	Emotion	Strategy	Did it Work?
Monday				
Tuesday				
Wednesday				
Thursday				
Friday				
Saturday				
Sunday				

Hopefully this activity has helped you find a strategy that works for you.

Weekly Activity:

As you've tried out different strategies during the week, you may have been able to foresee the challenges to being on time before they happen. For example, you may have known you tend to lose track of time when your friends message you. To avoid being distracted when time is short, you might have decided to turn off the notifications on your messaging app so you could get on with the task at hand.

We bet you were able to stop the challenge from being a problem on many occasions. That's awesome!

See if you can write down when you succeeded in pre-empting the challenge to being on time and stopped it before it slowed you down.

1.

2.

3.

4.

5.

6.

7.

You are getting really good at this. Awesome!

Did You Know…?

Did you know that astronaut Scott Kelly, who was the first American to spend a year in space, also has ADHD? He said he once thought he'd never be an astronaut because he couldn't concentrate in class. If Scott Kelly can spend a year in space, you can do anything you put your mind to!

Chapter Summary

- Being on time is difficult for people with ADHD because your brain tends to be easily distracted, which can make you forgetful.
- There are many strategies to help you with the challenges of being on time.
- Once you figure out the situations that make your ability to be on time difficult you can make sure they don't get in the way!

In the next chapter you will learn….

- Why people with ADHD have trouble with remembering.
- Strategies to help with the challenge of remembering.
- How to stop the situations that cause challenges to remembering.

SEVEN

Boosting My Memory

ARE you tired of forgetting things? It can be so annoying when you really mean to do something important, but it just slips your mind. People can get upset with you for forgetting to do things. It probably feels like your parents keep having to tell you to do the same things over and over again. They can't understand why you won't just do what they tell you.

Having ADHD means your memory doesn't work like everyone else's. That's why it's hard for you to remember to do your chores. It's why you lose things and leave things behind all the time, no matter how many times you tell yourself not to do it next time!

That must be so frustrating for you. You probably feel annoyed with yourself. It probably hurts that people get angry with you for forgetting things and losing things as if you do it on purpose. Try to write down some of the emotions you feel when facing the challenge of remembering things:

1.

2.

3.

4.

5.

6.

7.

Those are some difficult emotions to go through. Try not to worry. We have some possible solutions for you to try in order to help you remember the important things.

- **Make a daily timetable.** Timetables will help you remember what you have to do each day. Place anything you have planned for a set time in your timetable. For instance, homework, chores, school events (e.g. sports days) and plans with friends.

Show a parent your timetable for the next day so they can help you make sure you have everything you need for the day's plans. For instance, you might need to pack your gym clothes for sports day.

- **Make a checklist.** Are there some things you often forget? Make a checklist to ensure you don't leave these things behind. Whenever you are about to leave somewhere, check your list to make sure you have everything.

For instance, check for your jacket, phone, hat and shoes. You'd be surprised how many children—and some adults —leave their shoes behind after they've been playing in the park!

- **Keep objects in the same place.** ADHD makes it hard to focus. This means it's easy for you to pick something up and forget where you put it down, especially when your ADHD makes you distracted. By getting into the habit of putting your items in the same place every time you've finished with them, you reduce the likelihood of losing them.

For instance, if you consciously make sure to place your pens in a particular drawer in your desk, you will be more likely to place that pen in that place when you aren't thinking about it. If every object in your room has a designated place, not only will you keep your room tidy, but you'll be less likely to lose things.

- **Ask for help.** Talk to your teachers and parents about your challenge with remembering. If they know you struggle with this, they can help by reminding you.

For example, your teacher may notice if you leave something behind in class and give you a friendly reminder. If you include your parents and teachers as part of the solution, they will be more understanding when you struggle with remembering things.

- **Use visual triggers.** Even though you consult your timetable, you might get distracted before you manage to complete the task you were meant to do. A trigger will help remind you exactly what to do.

For instance, if it's your turn to feed the dog, place the feed bowl or container of food somewhere you will be likely to see it. You can also do this with a reminder note and put it somewhere you will see it, such as on the fridge. That way, as soon as you go to the fridge after school, you will remember to feed the dog.

Activity:

Do you have any other solutions that work for you in your challenge to remember things? Why don't you write them down?

1.

2.

3.

4.

5.

6.

7.

Daily Activity: Give it a Go:

Do you think any of the listed solution ideas might work for you? Why not try them out and see? Next time you're struggling with remembering to do things, or when you struggle to bring everything with you when you leave somewhere, try giving one of the above solutions a go.

Here's the example of how this might work:

Day	Cause	Emotion	Solution	Did it Work?
Monday	I keep forgetting to put the garbage out in the morning.	Frustration	Visual trigger	Yes, I placed my own waste paper bin in my doorway, which reminded me to take out the kitchen garbage.
Tuesday	I keep leaving my jacket at school.	Disappointment for letting my parents down	Check list	Yes, I checked my list before going home and remembered to get my jacket out of my locker before leaving.
Wednesday	I keep forgetting to do my math homework.	Anxiety	Daily timetable	Yes, my math homework was written down for a specific time after school, and looking at my timetable reminded me to do it.

Have you managed to try out some of the solutions for yourself? Excellent work! Fill out the table below to show which ones worked for you.

Day	Cause	Emotion	Solution	Did It Work?
Monday				
Tuesday				
Wednesday				
Thursday				
Friday				
Saturday				
Sunday				

Remember, not every solution will work or it may not work the first time. Don't lose faith if it takes time. You will get there in the end!

While you were testing out the solutions, did you notice any patterns? Perhaps you noticed certain situations which made remembering more challenging. We bet you can try to foresee some of these challenges and stop them before they happen. For instance, you might have found yourself more likely to leave things behind after school in your excitement to leave for the day.

In order to make sure you don't rush before giving yourself the chance to collect your things, maybe you could pause and make yourself wait. Try counting to five. This will slow you down giving you the chance to check and make sure you have everything you need.

Make a list of the instances where you managed to prevent yourself forgetting something:

1.

2.

3.

4.

5.

6.

7.

That's some list! Awesome. We bet your parents would love to see it. Show it to them and your teachers. They'll be excited to see your progress.

Did You Know...?

Did you know that famed gymnast Simone Biles has ADHD? Due to the difficulty of some of her routines, Simone Biles is thought to be one of the most talented gymnasts of all time.

In fact, some of her gym moves are so extreme, they were once thought to be impossible. Yet again, it seems, famous people with ADHD not only manage to overcome their symptoms, but they also manage to shatter expectations in their field of interest. People with ADHD *are* exceptional!

Chapter Summary

- ADHD makes it harder for people to remember things.
- There are many ways to help with the challenge of remembering. For example, daily planners ensure that every important task is listed so it won't be overlooked.
- Figuring out when a challenge to your memory is likely to occur will help you stop the challenge from happening.

In the next chapter you will learn....

- Why it's hard for people with ADHD to keep their cool sometimes.
- Strategies to help you when the challenge of being overwhelmed occurs.
- To predict the challenges to keeping your cool and help stop them from happening.

EIGHT

Keeping My Cool

IT'S easy to feel overwhelmed when you have ADHD. Not only do your own thoughts move very quickly, with lots of ideas competing in your head, but your hyperactivity makes it difficult for you to sit still and concentrate.

As well as the overwhelming nature of your own thoughts and feelings, the sights and sounds around you often become too much. This is because people with ADHD often have what's known as sensory overload.

Sometimes, people with ADHD can't block out sensory inputs. Sights and sounds are especially difficult for them to ignore. These sensations are often stronger in people with ADHD; sounds are louder, sights more vivid.

What emotions do you feel when faced with the challenge of staying in control? You might feel angry when people talk too much around you because the sound of their voices overwhelms you. Perhaps the stress of trying to figure out how to get everything done makes you upset.

You have so much to think of—your homework, your chores, extracurricular activities, and social engagements. It's no wonder you feel out of control sometimes! Your unique mind has difficulty focusing on one thing at a time. So, when you have a lot to do, you get a bit confused or even anxious.

Write down some of these emotions you are faced with when trying to deal with the challenge of keeping your cool.

1.

2.

3.

4.

5.

6.

7.

That's a lot to deal with. No wonder you feel a bit frazzled. Try not to worry though, we have some possible solutions for you to try to help you with the challenge of keeping your cool.

- **Calming measures.** If you are in a situation where sensory overload takes over or you simply can't cope, try to calm your response by counting to ten. If you are still feeling overwhelmed, try deep breathing exercises.

Breathe in slowly, counting as you breathe, hold your breath, and let it out slowly. Do this several times.

- **Use meditation.** If you are alone in your room or a quiet place, when panic takes over, try to meditate. There are many guided meditation apps that can guide you through meditation.

Meditation will empty your mind of thoughts. It will slow your mind down and allow you to be calm again.

- **Make a priority list.** If you have too many things to do, or too many thoughts and worries bombarding your mind at once, try to concentrate on only one thing.

Choose to think about the most important topic, or the thing that needs your attention first. Avoid the temptation to multitask when you are overwhelmed.

- **Listen to music.** If noises are causing sensory overload, block them out by listening to music. The music will have a calming effect and work to dampen the sound. Music will also help if you feel overwhelmed in general.

Pay close attention to the words and rhythm when you listen. Immersing yourself in the music will bring you back to the present moment and calm you down.

- **Do some exercise.** If you are unable to calm yourself, it may be best to remove yourself from the situation. A change of scene and moving your body will bring you back to a state of calmness.

Talk to your teacher about the need to remove yourself from class if you find yourself being overwhelmed. Going for a short walk might be all you need to reset your mind when everything seems like too much.

Activity:

Can you think of any more strategies you might use to stop this challenge? Write a few down:

1.

2.

3.

4.

5.

6.

7.

Daily Activity: Have a Go

Try out some of these things next time you're struggling to stay calm. Here is an example of how you might do this.

Day	Cause	Emotion	Strategy	Did it Work?
Monday	The noise of renovations next door made me upset and I couldn't concentrate on my homework.	Worked up, frustrated, and angry	Listen to music	Yes, it blocked out the sound and made me calm.
Tuesday	I became upset and confused thinking about my exams. I couldn't decide which one to study for first.	Angry, anxious	Prioritize	Yes, I chose to concentrate on just one subject and I was able to relax and get on with studying.

Try this for yourself in the table below:

Day	Cause	Emotion	Strategy	Did It Work?
Monday				
Tuesday				
Wednesday				
Thursday				
Friday				
Saturday				
Sunday				

Weekly Activity:

Hopefully as you've gone through the list of strategies you've managed to find a few that have worked for you. You've probably improved at guessing when you're likely to experience a challenge to your calmness. Well done! You're getting really good at this. You may even have managed to stop it from happening in the first place. For instance, you could have realized you are likely to get sensory overload when your brother or sister's friends come round. Before their noise gets to you, you could leave the room, thereby avoiding the feeling of being overwhelmed.

Try to write down the occasions when you've managed to stop the challenge to your calmness before it happens.

1.

2.

3.

4.

5.

6.

7.

Wow! You really *are* getting good at this! Keep up the good work. Now, we're sure your parents and teachers would like to see the latest list of your achievements. Why not show them now?

Did You Know…?

Did you know that Alexander Graham Bell was thought to have had ADHD? He had trouble in school, which we now know is probably down to ADHD. Despite this, he went on to invent the telephone! Having ADHD makes life hard for people, but it can also make them exceptional.

You are not alone in your struggles with ADHD. It may be that you have the same Super Skill as Alexander Graham Bell and have the imagination to invent great new things which change the world!

Chapter Summary

- It can be difficult for people with ADHD to keep their cool sometimes. This is because there is so much going on for people with ADHD. Their minds are so busy, they struggle with focus and everything around them seems to grab their attention. It can all feel like too much.
- There are many strategies to help people with ADHD keep their cool, such as calming measures, like counting to ten.
- If you can figure out when a challenge to keeping your cool might occur, you can stop it from happening.

In the next chapter you will learn....

- How to improve your social skills and your self-esteem.
- Strategies to help you boost your social skills and self-esteem.
- How to figure out when a challenge to your social skills and self-esteem is likely to occur so you can stop it from happening.

NINE

Boost My Social Skills and Increase Self-Esteem

GETTING on with people can be hard when you have ADHD. This is because impulsivity makes you so excited that you sometimes interrupt people when they're talking to you.

You may also find it hard to sit still and sometimes your energy can disrupt other people. Because you can have difficulty making friends, this can make you feel bad about yourself. Even though it's not your fault that you sometimes struggle in social situations, it's natural for you to feel a bit down if you have trouble making friends.

You can feel a lot of emotions when you struggle with being social. For instance, you might feel lonely, because you have trouble making friends. You may feel frustrated because someone may respond negatively when you are trying to express yourself in a way they think is inappropriate or loud.

Try to list how you feel when you struggle with social skills and self-esteem:

1.

2.

3.

4.

5.

6.

7.

That's a lot to deal with. Don't worry, we have some strategies you can try that might help.

- **Fidget toys.** If your hyperactivity puts people off, using a fidget toy may help to keep your energy in check.

Being able to sit still and stay quiet will help you relate to others in a way that they will find more appealing.

- **Counting.** If you are having a conversation with someone and you find yourself getting so excited about the topic that you feel the urge to interrupt, delay by counting to five.

By the time you've finished counting the urge to interrupt should have passed, allowing your conversational partner to finish what they are saying. When it's your turn to speak, you can talk about the idea that came to you.

- **Active listening.** When you talk to someone try to listen to every point they make. As attention is difficult for people with ADHD, this may be a challenge at first.

One way to help is to repeat the most important thing the other person says back to them. This shows them you are listening and helps you focus on the conversation. So you don't keep repeating a person's words back to them, at times repeat an important word in your head instead of voicing it aloud. Try to come up with a response to their speech, either a solution or an acknowledgement of what they have said.

For instance, if they say they have a headache, say you are sorry and offer a solution. You could suggest they drink some water in case they are dehydrated.

- **Use positive self-talk.** Sometimes people with ADHD can jump to the wrong conclusion and react emotionally without thinking things through. This is because ADHD makes you impulsive. When you have an issue with someone, try not to respond straight away.

For instance, if your friend doesn't answer your messages, don't get upset, thinking they are ignoring you. Instead of getting angry, wait. There is probably a good explanation, such as the fact that they may not have their phone on them.

- **Practice.** Practice your social skills by role playing with your family. Have a conversation with them and ask them to give you pointers afterward to let you know how you did.

Try using active listening. Hopefully your family will be delighted by what a good listener you have become!

- **Use positive thinking**. It's easy for people with ADHD to focus on negatives, because you're probably used to being told off because of your symptoms. Try to be your own cheerleader. If you have done well, congratulate yourself. The more you think about yourself doing well, the more likely you are to repeat this behavior.

Use positive affirmation, where you tell yourself out loud about one of your achievements. Imagine yourself doing things well. Think about how you can do well. This will help you try harder in all areas of life, which will, in turn, make you improve.

- **Don't compare.** It's hard not to compare yourself with your peers. But ADHD means that your brain is different, and therefore it's unfair for you to judge yourself against others. The most important thing is for you to be aware of your challenges and to continue to try to succeed in overcoming them.

It may take longer for you to do some things, but that's okay. As long as you try, you will be able to do anything! Also remember your Super Skills. Many of these skills actually make you better at some things than other children.

Activity:

We're sure this list has given you lots of ideas for solutions to the challenge of socializing and increasing your self-esteem. See if you can list some below:

1.

2.

3.

4.

5.

6.

7.

You really are becoming a pro at this. Great list! Let's see if you can put some of these great strategies to use.

Daily Activity: Have a Go

When you experience some of the emotions you identified as a result of your struggle with self-esteem and socializing, try some of the strategies discussed in this chapter.

4

Here's an example of how you might record this.

Day	Cause	Emotion	Strategy	Did It Work?
Monday	My best friend was talking when an idea came to me and I interrupted her.	Excited	Counting	Yes, I counted to five, which was difficult, but I managed to wait until my friend finished speaking before I took my turn.
Tuesday	My friend didn't want to go to the mall with me because she was busy. I saw her later at the mall with a group of other girls. I got upset and wanted to shout at her.	Jealous and sad	Positive self-talk	Yes, I told myself there might be a good reason for why she went with the other girls. It turned out she went to the mall with her boyfriend and was only saying hello to the other girls.
Wednesday	My friend is so much better at math than me and he doesn't study as much as I do. I'm stupid.	Frustrated and sad	Positive self-talk.	Yes, I tried to tell myself that math is not my thing. My brain is different and it takes me longer to learn some things. There are other things I'm better at than my friend.

Now see if you can fill out the below table in the same way.

Day	Cause	Emotion	Strategy	Did It Work?
Monday				
Tuesday				
Wednesday				
Thursday				
Friday				
Saturday				
Sunday				

Remember, don't feel bad if the strategies don't work straight away. It takes time and practice, but you will get there in the end.

Weekly Activity

Going through these strategies during the week, we're sure you've improved at figuring out when you might have your self-esteem and social skills challenged. You've probably managed to stop some of the challenges before they happen. Awesome! You're a star.

Share some of these victories below.

1.

2.

3.

4.

5.

6.

7.

Wow! You're doing a great job. We bet your teachers and parents will be looking forward to sharing your recent success. They will be proud when you show them this list.

Did You Know…?

Did you know that writer Jenny Lawson has ADHD? She described having low self-esteem as a child. She was shy and used writing as an outlet. In fact, Jenny became so good at writing that she went on to become a well known journalist and author. So, remember that even famous writers feel bad about themselves sometimes!

Chapter Summary

- Hyperactivity and impulsivity can make socializing difficult for people who have ADHD. This can result in low self-esteem.
- There are many strategies that can improve social skills, such as active listening.
- Figuring out when a challenge to socializing is likely to occur can stop it from happening.

In the next chapter you will learn....

- Why people with ADHD have trouble being organized.
- Strategies to help you overcome challenges to being organized.
- How to stop challenges to being organized.

TEN

Become Super Organized

ATTENTION AND HYPERACTIVITY issues make being organized a real challenge for people with ADHD. When everything around you captures your attention and you can't sit still, being on time, doing homework, and sticking to plans is difficult. It's hard to know what to do first when you have a long list of things to do.

Sometimes it can feel like too much, so you end up doing nothing at all. Then you end up feeling bad because you feel like you've failed. This can make you feel disappointed and sad.

How do you feel when being organized seems too hard? You might feel confused because you don't know where to start. You might feel anxious because you have so much homework to do and you don't seem to be getting anywhere. Due to your struggle to stay organized, you might end up handing in homework late, which makes you feel embarrassed or even ashamed.

Write down some of the feelings you have when you struggle with being organized.

1.

2.

3.

4.

5.

6.

7.

We're sorry you've experienced those feelings. It's a lot to deal with. Not to worry, we have some possible strategies for you to try.

- **Use a daily planner for homework.**
  Homework is such a big part of your life. It pays to dedicate a daily planner to it. Plan your week ahead by making note of the homework you need to do each day for every subject. If you do a little each day it will be easier to get your homework done.

Likewise, make a separate planner if you have any tests or exams. Try to make sure you set aside enough time to study all the information before your exams. Get a parent or teacher to help you with your planner. They can help you figure out how much time to spend on each topic, depending on the difficulty of the subject.

- **Have a dedicated work space.** Find a dedicated work space for homework. Set aside a comfortable place away from noise and devices.

Keep everything you need, like pens, paper, and exercise books close by. Turn off all devices when you work so you can concentrate on the task at hand.

- **Use a daily routine planner.** In your daily routine planner make note of everything you need to do in order to make your day run smoothly. Start with your morning routine and include everything you need to do to get ready, including brushing your teeth, placing your lunch in your bag and doing any morning chores.

Throughout the day, include the things you may need to do, like after school activities, including the time you plan to spend doing homework/studying.

Bedtime routines are important to ensure you get a good amount of sleep. Include things that help you relax and feel calm before going to sleep, like listening to music or meditation. Check your planner throughout the day.

You may need to set alarms to help you stick to the schedule.

- **Prioritize.** You need to decide what is more important between a variety of different tasks and actions. Learning to make priorities is an important life skill and not an easy one to learn.

Having ADHD means you are more inclined to want to do things that are rewarding and that make you feel good. Therefore, it takes more effort to do things that aren't so much fun.

When it comes to deciding how to spend your time, try to get the less exciting tasks done first. For instance, if you have a difficult project, you might naturally want to do everything else first. Try to do the hardest thing first. This will prevent you from delaying and will give you the chance to put in extra effort, if needed. Make a list of everything you need to do.

Try to figure out which things are more urgent. If they need to be done sooner, tackle them first. Some things have bigger rewards.

For instance, you should spend more time on a school project that is worth half of your final grade, than a project that is only worth a quarter of your final grade.

Ask a teacher or parent to help you figure out how much time to dedicate to each task if you have difficulty. They can help you figure out what to do first and how much time to spend on it.

Activity:

Can you think of any other strategies to help you when you are having trouble staying organized? List them here:

1.

2.

3.

4.

5.

6.

7.

Once more, you've come up with some great ideas. You're a star!

Daily Activity: Have A Go

Now that you have a lot of different strategies let's see if you can use them. Next time you find it difficult to stay organized, or if you struggle with how to prioritize, try out some of the solutions in this chapter.

In the table below are some examples of how to do this.

Day	Cause	Emotion	Strategy	Did It Work?
Monday	I have exams, and when I sat down to study, I became overwhelmed by how many subjects I had to learn about.	Anxious, nervous, and overwhelmed	Exam planner	Yes, my Mom helped me figure out a daily study planner. We made sure I studied each subject, spreading them over the whole week.
Tuesday	I tried to do my homework, but got distracted when I received a text message. I ended up texting my friends for so long, I ran out of time to study.	Disappointed and stressed	Dedicated work space	Yes, I turned off my phone so I didn't receive texts and turned off notifications on my social media. I was able to concentrate on studying so I managed to get my homework done.

See if you can fill out your own table below:

Day	Cause	Emotion	Strategy	Did It Work?
Monday				
Tuesday				
Wednesday				
Thursday				
Friday				
Saturday				
Sunday				

As you try out the strategies listed in this chapter, try to figure out when the challenge will happen in order to prevent it. For instance, you may realize that it's difficult to be organized when you've taken on too much. No matter how well you plan, there are only so many hours in the day.

So, if you know you have exams to study for, try not to plan for too many other things on the same day. If you go out for the day with your friends when you have to study, then you will probably not manage to get through all the revision you need to do. So, in order to make sure you can stick to your plans, arrange to see your friends on another day or for just an hour, which may be more manageable.

Make a list of the times when you managed to prevent challenges to being organized from happening, like the example above.

Awesome, you're starting to really get the hang of this. We bet your parents and teacher will also be impressed, so why not share your success with them?

Did You Know...?

Did you know that possibly the most famous basketball player of all time, Michael Jordan, has ADHD? It's amazing how many athletes have ADHD. It seems like the very best sports people, the ones who break all kinds of records, often have ADHD. There really is something special about the ADHD brain, isn't there? All that energy and hyper focus can definitely be used for amazing things.

Chapter Summary

- ADHD makes being organized difficult, due to symptoms like inattentiveness and hyperactivity.
- Strategies like a daily activity planner help remind you of what you need to do.
- Identifying the feelings you have when you struggle with being organized can help you stop being disorganized.

In the next chapter you will learn....

- Why sleep is difficult for people with ADHD and why it's also particularly important for you.
- Strategies to help you get enough sleep.
- To identify the emotions that come with your struggle to get enough sleep, so you can stop it from becoming a problem.

ELEVEN

Sleep Easy

SLEEP IS one of the most important things to help set you up for the day. Yet good sleep is one of the most difficult things for many people with ADHD to achieve. Hyperactivity and lack of attention means you are more likely to get to bed late.

When you do get to bed your mind probably runs at a hundred miles an hour, with lots of thoughts and ideas going around and around. You may also have very sensitive hearing. Noise may keep you awake. This is because your mind is more in tune with the things around you. This is one of your Super Skills, which means you are good at picking up on things before other people do.

For instance, you will be great in an emergency because you will see the need to help others before anyone else. When trying to sleep, however, you may have some difficulty. Loud noises, like people snoring or dogs barking, can disrupt your sleep.

So, it's hard for you to fall asleep for many reasons. What this means is you often wake up tired and irritable, which makes it really hard for you to get going first thing in the morning and can then make you tired during the day.

Not getting enough sleep causes a lot of frustration, and being tired all the time is no fun. How does it feel for you when you struggle to get enough sleep? You might feel anxious and worried as time goes by without falling asleep. You might end up sleeping in which means you end up rushing in the morning and forgetting things. This can make you feel stressed and upset.

Getting a good night of sleep is also crucial to managing ADHD symptoms. Lack of sleep can make you tired and cause symptoms like inattention to worsen. Some of the other things that happen as a result of ADHD, like forgetfulness and inability to focus, can also be made worse by lack of sleep.

Write down some of the feelings you experience when you struggle with the challenge of getting enough sleep.

1.

2.

3.

4.

5.

6.

7.

That sounds very stressful. Don't feel too upset. We have a few strategies to help you.

- **Have a bedtime routine**. Follow a strict bedtime routine listing everything you need to do before bed. ADHD means people become easily distracted and forgetful.

Many people with ADHD end up forgetting about getting to bed at a reasonable hour, and often miss out on doing things they need to do, such as brushing teeth.

Set specific times for each action. For example, if you need to get to bed by 8PM, you will need to have prepared things for the morning, brushed your teeth and changed into your pajamas before then. If you find yourself distracted, it may help to set an alarm to remind you of everything you need to do to prepare for bed.

- **Meditation.** Your mind may be too busy for you to fall asleep. Try simple meditation to calm yourself. Meditation will help you rid your mind of all thoughts. It will relax your body.

Try using a guided meditation app, which means you don't have to learn how to meditate before attempting to use this form of relaxation. All you have to do is listen.

- **Limit screen time.** The screens of devices are known to keep people from falling asleep. Try not to use your devices for at least half an hour before you go to bed.

You can also ask your parents to buy you some "blue blocker" glasses, which block out the light emitted by devices that are responsible for causing you to stay awake.

- **Listen to calming music.** Listening to music can help relax your mind, giving you the chance to forget about worries or stimulating thoughts.

Concentrate on the rhythm and how it makes you feel. Think of the music making your body heavy and relaxed. The calming nature of the music will help control hyperactivity, as well as prepare the mind for sleep.

- **Do some exercise.** If you have trouble sleeping try to do some exercise at least an hour before bed. This will burn off excess energy and is known to facilitate relaxation.

People who exercise in this way tend to fall asleep more quickly.

- **Have a massage.** There's nothing quite so relaxing as a massage. Ask a parent for a gentle shoulder massage. You could also use a massager if you have one.

Close your eyes and let the massage relax your body. You could find yourself falling asleep while you're getting a massage!

- **Take a warm bath**. Bathing in warm water often relaxes people. Put in some bubbles and sit back, relax, and let the warm water do its magic. Before you know it you'll be ready for a nice long sleep.

Can you come up with any solutions to try when you're challenged by getting enough sleep? List a few below.

1.

2.

3.

4.

5.

6.

7.

Wow! You've come up with some great ideas there. Now let's see if you can try some of these out for yourself.

Daily Activity: Have a Go

When you experience some of the emotions that occur when you have difficulty sleeping, try out some of the strategies discussed in this chapter. In the below table you will see how this might be done.

Day	Cause	Emotion	Strategy	Did it Work?
Monday	I couldn't sleep because there was too much going through my mind.	Stressed and tired	Guided meditation	Yes, it was easy because I used an app, which meant all I had to do was lay back and listen. I soon fell fast asleep.
Tuesday	I couldn't relax and fall asleep. I couldn't stop wanting to move my legs.	Wound up, fidgety	Listen to music	Yes, I chose calming music and tried to listen to all of the beats. Before I knew it, I didn't feel hyperactive anymore and fell asleep not long after.
Wednesday	I couldn't sleep because of the loud thunder outside.	Scared	Massage	Yes. My Mom gave me a shoulder massage that calmed me down. I ended up being too sleepy to be worried about the storm.

Now, see if you can try this for yourself in the table below:

Day	Cause	Emotion	Strategy	Did It Work?
Monday				
Tuesday				
Wednesday				
Thursday				
Friday				
Saturday				
Sunday				

Well done, you've put those strategies to good use. You're becoming a pro at this!

Weekly Activity

Now that you've tried out some of the strategies, we bet you've noticed some patterns developing around your sleep issues. You have probably been able to anticipate when challenges occur and have been able to stop them in their tracks. That's awesome. Why not list these successes below?

1.

2.

3.

4.

5.

6.

7.

That's great! Keep up the good work. Let your parents and teachers see your continued success.

Did You Know...?

Did you know that famous inventor Dean Kamen, who invented the Segway PT, said that it was his ADHD that led him to become such an accomplished inventor? It's because he had to find his own way of doing things that led him to come up with so many amazing ideas. Does that sound familiar?

If you have to do things your own way, you're not alone. Sometimes your way is the best way! The uniqueness of the ADHD brain really does help people to do amazing things.

Chapter Summary

- Sleep is difficult for people with ADHD due to symptoms like hyperactivity and tendencies to be sensitive to noise.
- There are many things to help you achieve better sleep, such as relaxing before bed in a warm bath.
- Identifying the emotions that come with not getting enough sleep can help you prevent the challenge from becoming worse.

In the next chapter you will learn....

- About the foods that will help decrease the unwanted symptoms of ADHD.
- Which foods people with ADHD should avoid.

TWELVE

Eat Well

WHAT YOU EAT CAN HAVE a huge impact on your ADHD symptoms. Many foods can increase your hyperactive tendencies. Others make it harder to concentrate, which only makes paying attention harder. There are however lots of foods which our brains love and which really help our brains to perform at their very best!

Let's look first at the foods we should include lots of in our diet.

Foods to Eat Frequently

Omega 3 Fatty Acids:

These are shown to improve the functioning of your brain and your concentration levels. This is very important for people with ADHD. Omega 3 fatty acids are the best thing for ADHD brains. It helps you concentrate and finish tasks. Omega 3 also happens to decrease restlessness, aggression, and hyperactivity. So, it's like a natural ADHD helper.

Foods high in omega-3 fatty acids: *salmon, mackerel, herring, avocado, flaxseed oil, tuna, olive oil, sardines, brazil nuts, walnuts, cod liver oil, flax seeds, chia seeds and soybeans.*

If you still aren't getting enough omega-3 fatty acids, there are some supplements available to give you an extra boost.

Protein:

Protein is a good source of energy for both the body and the mind. When you have ADHD you want to choose foods that will keep you going over a long period. Protein doesn't just give you steady energy, it also helps control hyperactivity.

· · ·

High-protein foods: *Nuts, beans, red and white meat (like chicken and beef), Greek yogurt, pumpkin seeds, fish, milk, broccoli, cauliflower, potatoes, peas, corn, kiwi, apricots, whole eggs, avocado, oats, cottage cheese, quinoa, and lentils.*

As you can see, some fruits and vegetables contain a high amount of protein. There are lots of yummy high-protein foods for you to choose from!

Complex Carbohydrates:

People often talk about avoiding carbohydrates because they are sugary. But not all carbs are bad; the best way to eat carbs is to choose brown (wholegrain) options instead of white (e.g., brown bread). Many natural sources of carbohydrates are also a good source of vitamins and the fiber in them can prevent sugar from being a problem.

Complex-carbohydrate foods: *Most vegetables and fruits but especially: sweet potato, squash, oranges, tangerines, pears, grapefruit, apples, kiwi, popcorn, brown rice, quinoa, barley, beans, brown bread, brown pasta, buckwheat, carrots, peas, strawberries, and oats.*

Yes, you read that right. Popcorn is a complex carb because it's a wholegrain.

Low GI (Glycemic Index):

Low GI foods cause a slow release of energy which is the best way to avoid energy spikes and help to control hyperactivity.

Low GI foods: Wholegrain and multigrain bread, steel cut oats, wholegrain basmati rice, some fruit, vegetables, beans and dairy products.

Foods to Avoid:

It's best to try to avoid foods that contain additives and sugar as these cause sugar rushes and energy spikes. They also tend to result in an energy crash and sugar withdrawal, which can give you headaches, fatigue and irritability, none of which is good for concentration and mood.

Try to avoid the following foods: candy, corn syrup, sugar, skinless white potatoes, fries, white flour in cakes, white bread, pasta and artificial additives.

Sometimes it's hard to guess which foods contain sugar or additives. If in doubt, ask a parent to help you.

A healthy diet should include lots of fresh fruits and

vegetables, wholegrain carbohydrates, protein and good fats (omega 3). If you eat a lot of fruit and vegetables, you're more inclined to get a good range of vitamins, which are really important for growth, development and positive mood. If you eat fish twice a week, you should get a good amount of omega-3, which is the food your brain loves the most!

Daily Activity: Have a Go

See if you notice how certain foods affect your mood or ability to concentrate.

Perhaps start a little food diary to document what you are eating and note down anything specific you notice about your mood that day. e.g. you might notice that shortly after eating lots of chocolate you have uncontrollable energy, can't sit still in class and keep interrupting the teacher.

Did You Know...?

Did you know that Dave Grohl, front liner for The Foo Fighters, struggled to maintain his focus in school due to ADHD? He's one of many musicians who suffer from ADHD. It just goes to show that the creative side of ADHD can result in some really talented individuals.

Chapter Summary

- Try to avoid foods high in sugar and additives because they can exacerbate ADHD symptoms, like hyperactivity.
- Healthy foods like those high in protein, omega-3 fatty acids, and complex carbohydrates help improve concentration and decrease ADHD symptoms like lack of focus.
- A balanced diet with lots of natural fresh foods can help make the things you don't like about ADHD much less of a problem.

In the next chapter you will learn....

- How medication can help.
- When you may need medication.
- Who to see about medication.
- What you can do to make medication work best.

THIRTEEN

Medication and Me

ADHD MEANS your brain works a little differently to other people's brains. A lot of the time this is great as it makes you a unique and interesting individual. Sometimes though it can make everyday things a bit of a struggle for you. When these struggles become too much it may be time to consider medication.

Medication works to help control some of the symptoms of ADHD so they don't disrupt your life too much. It does this by helping the chemicals in your brain that are affected by ADHD work a bit better.

Studies[1] have shown that medication can reduce all of the main symptoms of ADHD, including hyperactivity, impulsivity, and lack of focus. This means medication can make it easier to do things like sit still, think through your decisions before you act, and focus.

Does Medication Really Work?

Studies show that ADHD medication will help 80% of people who take it. Medication is most effective when used alongside other lifestyle changes and coping strategies, like the ones you've already been practicing in this book.

People who take medication for ADHD have reported improvements in the following areas:

- Increased ability to concentrate. They found they were able to sit down and spend more time on tasks they did not find stimulating.
- Impulse control. People found medication helped them control impulses better. They reported an increased ability to think before acting.
- Better organizational skills. People reported that medication helped them not only stay on task, but also complete tasks.

Medication does not control all of the symptoms of ADHD. Many people who take medication still experience some of the following symptoms:

- Emotional challenges. Some people with ADHD still struggle with their emotions when taking medication.

- Forgetfulness. Despite helping people be more focused, people still describe having difficulty remembering things even when they are taking medication.
- Lateness. Some people still reported difficulty being on time even when taking medication.

What this means is that, although medication helps some of the main symptoms of ADHD, it doesn't fix everything. This is why it's important to include coping strategies in your management plan for ADHD. What medication does is help to control your symptoms so that it's easier for you to put strategies and lifestyle changes to use.

Let's recap some of the lifestyle changes we've mentioned in this book that will be useful alongside medication:

- Healthy eating
- Exercising
- Getting enough sleep

Now, let's recap some of the strategies you've used in this book that will help you alongside taking medication:

- Social-skills training (for example, active listening)
- Meditation
- Daily planners
- Fidget toys

When to take medication:

If you've found lifestyle changes and behavioral strategies aren't enough to help you overcome your ADHD, it may be time for you to think about medication.

There are a few signs that you may need a bit of extra help in the form of medication.

1. You are unable to concentrate or sit still even though you've tried all kinds of strategies to overcome these symptoms.
2. You feel upset and emotional a lot of the time and relaxation/calming measures don't seem to help.
3. Your behavior is disruptive despite your attempts to stop your hyperactive symptoms
4. You feel like your own behavior is out of control and you're fed up.
5. You're sad because your symptoms get in the way of making friends.

How to get medication:

The first step is to make an appointment with your GP. They can put you in touch with a psychiatrist or clinical psychologist who can then help get you started on your medication. Some of these specialists will be used to dealing with different age groups and your GP should be able to point you in the direction of the right one for you.

How to take medication:

People with ADHD sometimes have trouble taking medication. The senses of people with ADHD can be heightened. The sense of taste or the feel of pills can cause discomfort.

If you find pills hard to swallow there are a few different approaches you can ask about, including capsules that can be opened and sprinkled on food. It's important to take your medication regularly in order for it to work. Add medication to your daily planner. As long as you get into the habit of checking everything off on your daily list, you're sure to never miss taking a pill.

What if medication changes your personality?

Medication for ADHD will only make some of the symptoms decrease. It won't change who you are. You will still be you. Medication doesn't change or remove the symptoms of ADHD; it just controls them a little.

Think of ADHD as being a really bright light. Sometimes your ADHD light shines a bit too bright. Medication won't remove the light, but it will turn it down a bit so that it's not too overwhelming. The good things about ADHD, your Super Skills, most likely won't be affected by medication. You'll still be adventurous, fun, spontaneous, and all of the other wonderful things about ADHD that make you awesome.

There are a few different kinds of medication. Your practitioner will be able to help you decide which is best for you. Some people who have ADHD are also diagnosed with other disorders, like depression or obsessive-compulsive disorder (OCD). Some ADHD medications are also useful in treating other disorders as well. If you think you may be suffering from something other than ADHD, like depression, your practitioner will be able to help treat this as well.

Side Effects:

It's natural to be worried about side effects. Most side effects won't be too bad, and will probably go away after a while. You will be started on a small dose and your reaction will be monitored closely. Take note of your own reaction yourself.

Try to considering the following:

- Have your ADHD symptoms improved or worsened over time?
- Are there any side effects? For example, headaches, loss of appetite, or sore tummy?
- Have your moods changed? Are you sadder than usual?

If you are worried, get in touch with your doctor to discuss whether your medication needs changing or the dose has to be adjusted. Ask your parents to take note of how you seem when on medication. There may be some things they notice of which you aren't aware.

Therapy and Medication

Most likely you will be offered the chance to treat your ADHD with therapy alongside medication. Medication works better alongside behavioral strategies and therapy is one of the best strategies you can try.

A qualified therapist can help you with your behavior strategies and will be able to give you lots of ideas about how you can overcome the symptoms of ADHD.

Sometimes, just talking to someone you don't know very well can help, especially when that person is an expert whose knowledge and advice you can trust.

Remember, if you go on medication it doesn't need to be

forever. Most people's ADHD symptoms decrease as they age. Medication is intended to help you when you are struggling with your symptoms so you can get on with being who you are meant to be.

Did You Know...?

Did you know that *Dancing with the Stars* performer, Karina Smirnoff, says that improvements in the symptoms of her ADHD meant she can focus better and see things through to the finish?

Her ADHD still gives her the energy to work long hours practicing dance routines. If you ever feel like your symptoms are a balancing act, remember superstars like Karina Smirnoff struggle with this too! You are not alone.

Chapter Summary

- Medication can help decrease symptoms like hyperactivity and inattentiveness.
- Medication works best when paired with lifestyle strategies.
- Therapy is a particularly helpful strategy to use alongside medication.

In the next chapter you will learn....

- How to explain ADHD to other people so they understand what ADHD is and what it isn't.
- To help people realize you are different and that it's not your fault.
- To let people know when you need help with your struggles.

---

1. "The Facts on ADHD Medications | Child Mind Institute." https://childmind.org/article/the-facts-on-adhd-medications/. Accessed 10 Mar. 2021.

FOURTEEN

Explaining ADHD to Others

PEOPLE HAVE a lot of different ideas about ADHD. Most people understand that people with ADHD have trouble keeping still and paying attention. But there are a lot of things about ADHD they don't understand. Sometimes people think all you need to do in order to stop being hyperactive is to make yourself sit still, or that the best way for you to pay attention is just to snap out of daydreaming and try harder to focus. If only it were that simple!

People sometimes think you are being disruptive on purpose when it's not your fault that ADHD makes it so difficult for you to sit still.

The best way to explain ADHD to other people is to be honest. Tell them the facts. Keep it real and use facts.

Things you can tell people about your ADHD:

- Our ADHD brains work slightly differently than other people's brains. This is why we're different as well.

- As our brains work differently we find some things more challenging than people without ADHD.

For example we can find it hard to focus or sit still and struggle to stay organized and remember things.

- Equally, the different way in which our brain works also means we find some things much easier than people without ADHD.

For example, we are often very creative and adventurous. We are full of energy so we are lots of fun too.

- Super Skills is the name we give to the many positives of ADHD. There are so many of them! We are often hyper focused, which means we are able to focus on a specific thing really well.

We are also very caring, which makes us great friends. Being so energetic often makes us brilliant at sport too.

- ADHD affects many areas of our life and behavior. It's not just about running around or not being able to listen for long periods.

We sometimes struggle to make friends and find it hard to get to sleep, which often makes us tired and emotional.

- We are always learning about our symptoms and finding ways to overcome any difficulties.
- Having ADHD can mean we feel overwhelmed by things around us.

These include loud noise, busy places or lots of activity.

- If we are being loud or interrupting others, we usually aren't doing it on purpose, we just have so much we want to say. We find it really difficult not to blurt it all out.

- ADHD does not make us less intelligent, in fact we are very bright. It just means our brain works a bit differently so we need to do things a bit differently to get the same result.

We can do anything anyone else can. In fact there are many things we can do better than people without ADHD.

- We have lots and lots of little tips and tricks to help us with the things we find challenging.

This makes them much less of a problem.

- Although it may be difficult to tell us if we upset you, we always prefer if you are honest with us and tell us how you feel. For example, if we do something that is disruptive you should tell us so that we can use some of the tips and tricks we know to help us be less disruptive and that way we can stay really good friends.

Likewise, it helps us if you listen to what we find difficult too, for example loud noises or crowded places.

- As we grow we will find that our symptoms naturally decrease and we outgrow some of our ADHD.

Daily Activity: Have a Go

Can you think of anything else you might tell someone about your ADHD? Maybe you could keep a diary and write down things that you discover that people don't know about ADHD. That way, when you meet someone new you can be sure to tell them about it so that it doesn't cause any frustrations between you.

Your ADHD makes you unique. Your Super Skills make you outstanding. When people get to know you they are sure to appreciate you and the good things about you. Don't be afraid to tell them about yourself.

If people know you are struggling because of ADHD they will be more understanding when you have issues. Most people will want to help you if you tell them you are having difficulty.

Did You Know...?

Did you know that when *America's Got Talent's* host, Howie Mandel, publicly admitted to having ADHD he was really worried about what people would think? Well, he needn't have worried because people were very understanding and supportive. Like Mandel, you shouldn't worry about what people think of your ADHD.

Chapter Summary

- Being honest about ADHD will help people realize why you have the symptoms you do.
- Letting people know when you are struggling with ADHD will help them understand you better.

In the next chapter you will learn....

- 10 forms of meditation you can try, which will help you with your symptoms.

FIFTEEN

10 Meditations to Try

MEDITATION HAS SO many uses for people with ADHD. It can help control hyperactivity, increase focus, and improve decision making. With meditation you can start to solve sleep problems so that late nights and accidental sleep-ins are a thing of the past.

Meditation can help you calm your emotions and balance out your moods. Hopefully you've already given meditation a go so you know how good it can be. If not, now is a great time to start!

There are many different types of meditation. Some are simple and quick, which are good to use when you're in a hurry. Others are designed to help you get to as deep a state of relaxation as possible.

We've come up with ten meditations for you. Why not try them all?

1. Body Scan Meditation. Sit or lay down in a comfortable position and close your eyes. Scan your body from your toes to your head. Starting at your toes, take note of how they feel. Are they cold or hot? Move up your calf muscles and note how they feel. Are they tight or warm?

Keep going up your body, up your legs, hips, stomach and chest all the way to the top of your head. Taking the time to feel each body part will take your mind away from everything else, allowing you to relax.

2. Muscle Tension Meditation. Scan your body like in the previous exercise, but this time squeeze each body part, holding it for a few seconds before releasing and moving on to the next body part.

The contrast between tightening and relaxing will allow you to relax even more deeply.

3. Counting Meditation. Counting is used to take your mind away from distractions. Empty your mind of thoughts and start to count backward slowly. Try not to think of anything else or listen to sounds around you. If counting is too easy try subtracting in multiples of two.

For instance start at 100 and subtract two, to get 98.

Then subtract two again to get 96. Keep going until you feel completely relaxed. If you're a math whiz try subtracting by other numbers like three or four.

4. Sound Meditation. Start meditating by closing your eyes and listening to sounds that are close by. Concentrate on what you hear in the room like creaking floor boards or the buzz of the refrigerator. Push your sense of hearing further out across the room and then to just outside the window to take in sounds like birds chirping and trees rustling.

Push your hearing out further to listen to vehicles on the road, then further still to hear the sound of traffic far away.

5. Deep Breathing Meditation. Place a hand on your stomach and breathe in deeply, counting slowly until you can't count any further. Hold your breath for a short count and then let it out counting slowly as you go.

Try to inflate your lower lungs by feeling your stomach rise. With practice, you will be able to count your breaths in and out for longer, achieving deeper relaxation.

6. Guided Meditation. You can do guided meditation by following a recording or through in-person meditation. The usefulness of guided meditation is that you don't have to do anything other than follow another person's voice.

They will guide you through meditation by using various techniques; all you have to do is close your eyes and relax.

7. Kindness Meditation. This is one of the most positive types of mindfulness you can try. In this meditation, try to send out positive thoughts and kindness to the world. You can send out positive vibes to the world in general, or to specific people, pets, or even places or nations.

It's said that when you send out positivity you will improve your own happiness.

8. Transcendental Meditation. This meditation is used to transcend or improve your state of being. It uses a mantra, which is a saying that is repeated while relaxing and breathing deeply. You can be given a mantra by an instructor, or choose one yourself. Such as, "I will be kinder to people."

Saying it over and over will bring you to a relaxed state and might even help you achieve the goal of the mantra!

9. Visualization Meditation. Start meditating by relaxing and breathing deeply. Choose something visual to focus on. It can be anything you like: an object, like an apple, or the sky. Try to visualize everything about the object.

For instance, if it's an apple, think of the color, the smoothness, the shine, or any blemishes it may have. You can also start to imagine other sensations, like the feel of the object. This meditation activates a specific part of the brain, releasing other parts of the brain and allowing your mind to relax.

10. Sound Bath Meditation. Using a recording or in person, use a series of sounds to trigger relaxation. The sounds you meditate on include gongs and bowls which are banged and tapped to make unique relaxing sounds. The more you meditate in this way the more your body and mind will learn to relax to the sounds.

These are just some of the meditations you can try. Some may suit you, others may not. Some may suit a particular mood you have. They may have many different outcomes. Some make you relaxed. Others may make you feel creative or energized. Experiment. Try out a few and see which ones are best for you or the mood you're in at the time.

Did You Know…?

Did you know rapper will.i.am says the positive traits (Super Skills) of ADHD help him when he's writing music? Use your own Super Skills and you can be successful too!

Chapter Summary

- There are many different kinds of meditations you can try. Choose whichever suits you best.
- Meditation has many benefits, such as relaxation and improved mood.

In the next chapter you will learn….

- 10 exercises to help you stop being hyperactive.
- How to choose the exercises that suit people with ADHD.

SIXTEEN

10 Exercises to Reduce Fidgeting

EXERCISE IS one of the best things you can do to help with your ADHD symptoms. Not only does exercise burn off energy, but your brain releases positive chemicals when you exercise. Boosting these "feel good" chemicals in the brain is known to decrease the symptoms of ADHD. So, exercise will benefit you in many ways.

1. Walking. This is one of the most convenient types of exercise that you can try. It doesn't require special equipment, apart from a good pair of shoes. It can fit into your lifestyle perfectly.

It is said to be one of the best forms of exercise for you because it is low-impact and it is also relaxing. Walking to school will help burn off a little bit of energy, setting you up for the day.

2. Horseback riding. Horseback riding has been used as therapy for children with ADHD for many years. The benefits of horseback riding for people with ADHD go beyond the mere physical aspects. Learning to ride is all about balance, not just of your body but also your mind.

You have to consider not just the correct riding positions, but also the fact that you have to interact with a living, feeling being. This teaches you about communication, and how your emotions affect others. Horses pick up on your moods and often reflect them back to you, which is a good way to teach you to be calm.

3. Swimming. This is an excellent exercise for people with ADHD. This is because the environment, sights and sounds in particular, can be more vivid to people with ADHD. Water is calming because it mutes sounds. It helps people with ADHD get away from the distractions of the world. It's also refreshing and fun.

You can certainly get rid of a case of the fidgets easily by splashing and jumping about in water.

4. Martial arts. Martial arts are brilliant for confidence. Getting stronger and being able to defend yourself is great for self-esteem, which people with ADHD sometimes lack. Practicing martial arts is a good way to make friends.

Going through the grades together will bring you closer to people at your level.

5. Yoga. Yoga is about flexibility and strength. The moves can be very physical and are an excellent way of burning off energy.

There's also a meditative aspect to yoga, which includes deep breathing and holding poses. You already know how good meditation is for you!

6. Kayaking. Your ADHD makes you adventurous. Rushing down a river in a kayak is a great way to burn a bit of extra energy and it's fun for children who like adventure.

Just be sure to get a good guide and you can paddle your way to calmness.

7. Dance. Dance is a great way to get rid of excess energy. It also requires coordination and learning to follow directions, both of which will improve your focus.

Dancing is also great for getting in touch with your feelings. Dance allows you to express yourself and helps you work through your emotions.

.   .   .

8. Trampolining. Let's face it, it's almost impossible not to have fun when bouncing on a trampoline. Your ADHD makes you fun-loving and this is the perfect sport to keep you smiling and burning energy.

9. Hiking. This form of exercise has the benefit of bringing you closer to nature.

Being amongst the trees and fresh air will refresh you and have just the kind of calming effect you need.

10. Rock-climbing. We had to add another adventurous exercise just for you. It takes concentration and good decision making to climb more difficult indoor and outdoor climbing walls. You'll love the adrenaline rush that comes with being high in the air.

Whatever exercise you do, the best thing for you is to have fun! Use your extreme energy, Super Skills, and your amazing spirit of adventure to try something new.

Did You Know...?

Did you know Super Bowl champion, Terry Bradshaw, turned to sport after struggling at school? He went on to do incredibly well. You may also find school difficult sometimes and if Terry Bradshaw struggled at school that proves you are not alone. You also can overcome your ADHD challenges and take advantage of your Super Skills.

Chapter Summary

- Different forms of exercise will help with the symptoms you experience.

In the next chapter you will learn....

- 5 tips that will help you with your homework.

SEVENTEEN

5 Homework Tips and Tricks

HOMEWORK ISN'T the easiest thing in the world for people with ADHD. With your attention challenges, hyperactivity, and impulsiveness, that makes you want to do fun things, just sitting still can be difficult. Here are a few tips to help you get over your homework heartache:

1. Find a quiet, comfy space. Dedicate a space for homework. Make sure it is away from distractions like television and devices. Ensure the chair you sit in is comfortable and that you are warm and there is some fresh air through a window.

If you don't feel like being in the room where you do your homework, you're less likely to stay there for very long.

2. Break It Up. Sitting for long periods struggling with homework will only make your hyperactivity and struggles with attention worse.

Break your homework into smaller parts and aim to do 20 minutes followed by a 5 minute break. Leave the room and do something fun, ideally outside in the fresh air.

3. Homework Chart. In a chart, write down the homework you need to do every day for each subject. Choose a specific time for homework each day when you know you won't be disturbed or too tired. Once you have completed your homework for each day, tick it off. That way all you need to do is look at your daily homework chart to see where you're at.

4. Do your homework early. Putting less fun things off in favor of exciting or entertaining choices is something all children have a tendency to do, but for those with ADHD this tendency is even stronger.

Often people with ADHD put off their least favorite tasks until it's too late to do them! Avoid this outcome by doing your homework as soon as possible. It's also much better to tackle your homework before you become too tired towards the end of the day.

5. Reward yourself. Once you've completed one piece of homework reward yourself. Make the reward something you really enjoy or want, such as time playing your favorite video games or streaming your favorite series.

People with ADHD are often more motivated by positive experiences. Take advantage of this fact and use your own fun-loving nature to reward and motivate your good work.

Did You Know...?

Did you know that famous heiress, Paris Hilton, has struggled with ADHD? People's lives may sometimes seem perfect, but everyone has difficulty sometimes. ADHD can affect people from all kinds of backgrounds.

Chapter Summary

- Homework can be difficult for people who have ADHD.
- There are many things you can do to help make homework easier (e.g. homework planners).

In the next chapter you will learn....

- Who to talk to if you feel worried about ADHD.
- That there are a lot of different people in your life who are able to guide you.

EIGHTEEN

Who to Go to If I Feel Worried or Want Some Help Managing My ADHD

ADHD MAKES YOU UNIQUE. You feel so much. You are so brave and adventurous. You live life to the full and you are always on the go. Sometimes living life with extreme emotions can feel like too much to cope with. When this happens there are lots of people you can reach out to.

- **Parents.** Your parents love you and they want what's best for you. You may feel like your parents have been through enough trying to help you with your symptoms and struggles with ADHD. Maybe you don't want to trouble them anymore. Maybe you don't want to disappoint them.

Trust us, if you are brave enough to go to your parents and ask for their help, they will be proud of you.

- **Siblings.** Sometimes you argue. Sometimes your brother or sister are a pain, but they may also be your closest friends. If they're close enough in age, they'll understand some of the things you're going through with school, puberty and growing up.

They probably also know you really well and you can probably tell them anything. When it comes to serious problems most siblings can be your biggest helpers.

- **Grandparents**. The special relationship you have with your grandparents makes them ideal sounding boards. They are not as deeply involved in your day-to-day life as your parents so it can be easier to talk to them.

Grandparents are usually very wise as they have years of experience from all sorts of things in life.

- **Friends.** Friends are some of the people who know you best. Good friends want each other to be happy. They probably think you're pretty great, which is why you're friends!

So, don't be afraid to tell them how you feel and reach out for help.

- **Teachers.** They see you every day and all they really want is for you to do well.

If you confide in your teachers they will probably do everything they can to help you.

- **Coaches.** A sports coach is good to talk to for more than just game tactics. Often a coach is a motivational and caring kind of person. They are good at understanding the concerns of teens and children.

You may find a coach is easier to talk to than some other adults. If you have a good relationship with your coach they may be able to give you good, down-to-earth advice.

- **Doctors.** Your GP can give you general information and point you in the direction of specialists who can help with your situation.

GPs are a great place to start when finding out who to talk to about your symptoms and feelings about ADHD.

- **Psychologists/psychiatrists/specialists.** No matter where you're at in your treatment for ADHD, you can always speak to your psychologist/psychiatrist or other specialist. Even if you've just recently had an appointment you can go back to them if you need some extra help or advice.

These experts are used to all kinds of problems associated with ADHD. They have likely dealt with all kinds of problems that arise as a result of ADHD symptoms and they are usually great listeners.

- **Guidance counselors.** ADHD is often difficult to deal with in a school setting. If you feel like you can't wait to talk to someone about your concerns and you don't feel comfortable talking to a teacher, guidance counselors are a good alternative.

They are trained to deal with issues like ADHD and can be a good resource for you in a high-stress school environment.

- **Religious leaders.** If you follow any faith, a leader of your community may be good to talk to. For instance, it's part of a priest's and rabbi's job to give thoughtful and kind guidance to their followers.

If you would like some more information or support there are plenty of trusted websites you can go to that will offer nonjudgmental, expert advice. https://www. additudemag.com/ is a fact-filled site that has information about ADHD for people of all ages and perspectives. https://www.verywellmind.com/ is a site dedicated to general mental health conditions and is a good resource for ADHD.

The country you live in will have an organization dedicated to ADHD. For instance, here is one for the US: https://chadd.org/. This site is suitable for people of different ages and backgrounds including your parents and other professionals. If you're in the UK, you can go here https://www.adhdfoundation.org.uk/.

Did You Know…?

Did you know that Leonardo Da Vinci used the ADHD Super Skill of creativity to paint the most famous painting in the world, the *Mona Lisa*? He also invented a lot of incredible things, like flying machines and a helicopter. If you tap into your Super Skills you too can achieve incredible things!

Chapter Summary

- There are many people who can help you with ADHD (e.g. grandparents and guidance counselors).
- Websites dedicated to ADHD have a lot of resources to help you learn about ADHD and support you and your family.

Final Words

YOU'VE DONE IT! You've reached the end of this book. You've learned so much and done such excellent work. You should be so proud of yourself and so should your family and teachers. Make sure you share this achievement with them and show them how far you have come in your ADHD journey.

So, what now? Well, all the things you've learned in this book, the strategies you've used and the things you've discovered about your Super Skills will all be useful to you in your ADHD journey from here on. If you do find yourself struggling with the symptoms of ADHD you can use the lessons you've learned here to help you.

You may still struggle with things like hyperactivity, lack of focus, getting enough sleep, being late, making friends and making the right decisions, but you've learned so many strategies you can use to help you with all of these problems.

One of the aims of this book is to help you figure out how to help yourself when ADHD challenges you. You have identified many of the emotions you have when you are challenged by ADHD and you've learned how to stop those challenges before they go too far. You can continue to do this from now on. You can hopefully come up with strategies of your own for any new challenges you have.

Have faith in yourself! You can take control of your own future using what you've learned in this book. Don't forget though, on the days you may feel overwhelmed or like you just need to talk about your struggles, there are lots of people you can turn to for friendly advice. You just need to ask.

You know by now that you have incredible Super Skills, that make you better than other people at so many things. Your ADHD can make you creative. You have a limitless imagination and you have so much energy and focus that you'll never give up when you put your mind to something.

Use your Super Skills to your advantage and there's no limit to what you can achieve. Remember all the famous people we learned about who have ADHD and all the great things they achieved; you too can achieve incredible things. Maybe your name will appear at the Olympics or as the inventor of something amazing. Whatever you want to do, however big or small, just keep believing in yourself and you will succeed!

All the best of luck as you continue your ADHD journey. Keep this book to refer to throughout your journey so you always have help if you forget some of the things you have learned.

Continue to use the tips and tricks you've worked on to help manage your ADHD, eat lots of brain food, exercise daily and sleep like an angel. Look after yourself and your amazing brain will love you back 100 times over. Stay unique, aim for the stars, and you will go far.

Made in the USA
Columbia, SC
05 May 2025

57574465R00089